Straight and Curving

Sue Barraclough

Heinemann
LIBRARY

www.heinemann.co.uk/library
Visit our website to find out more information about **Heinemann Library** books.

To order:
☎ Phone 44 (0) 1865 888066
🖹 Send a fax to 44 (0) 1865 314091
🖥 Visit the Heinemann Bookshop at www.heinemann.co.uk/library to browse our catalogue and order online.

First published in Great Britain by
Heinemann Library, Halley Court, Jordan Hill,
Oxford OX2 8EJ, part of Harcourt Education.
Heinemann is a registered trademark of Harcourt
Education Ltd.

Editorial: Dan Nunn and Stig Vatland
Design: Jo Hinton-Malivoire and Bigtop
Picture Research: Ruth Blair, Erica Newbery and
Kay Altwegg
Production: Duncan Gilbert

Originated by Chroma Graphics (Overseas) Pte. Ltd
Printed and bound in China by South China
Printing Company

10 digit ISBN 0 431 02426 X
13 digit ISBN 978 0 431 02426 4

10 09 08 07 06
10 9 8 7 6 5 4 3 2 1

British Library Cataloguing in Publication Data
Barraclough, Sue
  Straight and curving. - (How do things move?)
  1.Momentum (Mechanics) - Juvenile literature
  I.Title
  531.1'12
A full catalogue record for this book is available
from the British Library.

Acknowledgements
The publishers would like to thank the following
for permission to reproduce photographs:
Alamy Images pp. **11, 23 top left** (Bertrand
Collet), **13** (Royalty-Free), **16** (Stockbyte
Platinum); Corbis pp. **4, 8**; Corbis pp. **12, 20, 22
top right, 23 top right** (Royalty free), **15, 22
bottom** (Ariel Skelley), **18** (Tom Stewart), **21, 23
bottom** (Robert Pickett); Digital Vision p. **9**
(Robert Harding World Imagery/Jim Reed); Getty
Images pp. **5, 6, 7** (Photodisc); Harcourt
Education Ltd (Tudor Photography) pp. **14, 22
top left**; Photographers Direct p. **17** (Skyscan);
Superstock p. **10** (Raymond Forbes); Trip p. **19**
(Art Directors).

Cover photograph reproduced with permission of
Alamy (Epictura).

Every effort has been made to contact copyright
holders of any material reproduced in this book.
Any omissions will be rectified in subsequent
printings if notice is given to the publishers.

The paper used to print this book comes from
sustainable resources.

Contents

Straight

These pieces of spaghetti are all **straight**.

straight

The pencils and ruler
are all **straight** too.

Curved

curve

These things are both **curved**.

Can you follow the **curves** on this bridge with your finger?

Straight and curved

Are these flagpoles
straight or **curved**?

Is this rainbow **straight**
or **curved**?

Moving straight

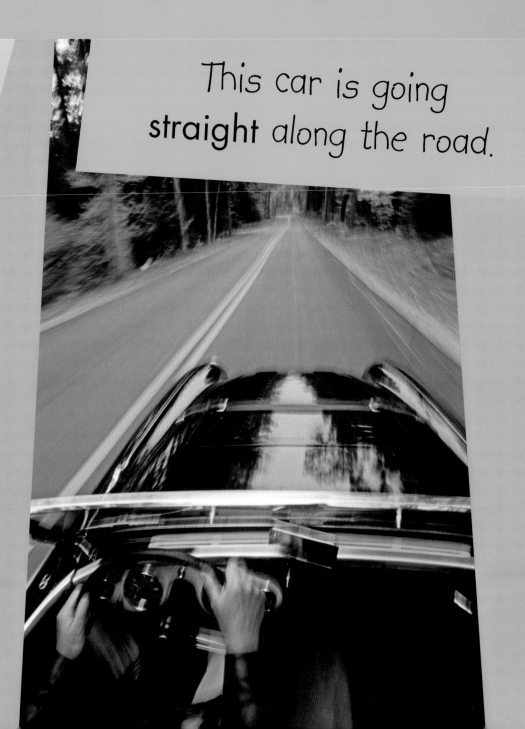

This car is going straight along the road.

These aeroplanes are flying
straight in the sky.

Curving around

This girl is following the **curve** in the path.

This skateboarder is zooming around the **curves** in the path.

Sliding down

This slide is **straight**.
The girl is going **straight** down the slide.

This slide has many **curves**.

The girl is **curving**
down the slide.

Up in the sky

This kite is flying high in the sky.

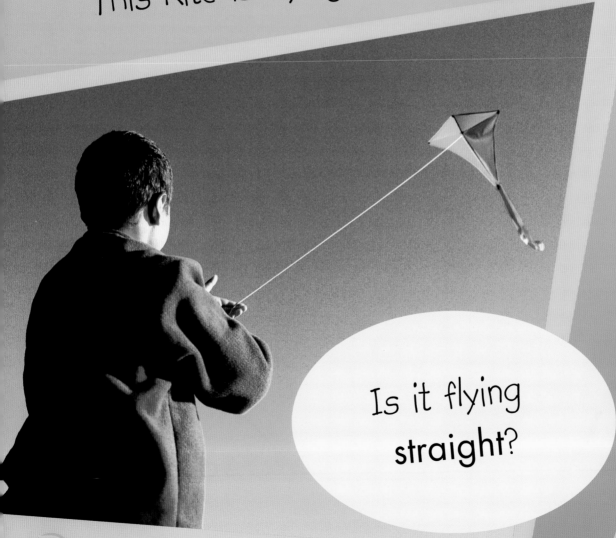

Is it flying straight?

Is this kite flying straight or is it curving?

Fun and games

This girl is sliding down the pole.
Is she moving straight?

These cars are racing around the track.

Are they moving straight or are they curving?

Plants and animals

This sunflower is growing tall and strong.

Is it growing straight?

This worm is moving along the ground.

Is it moving straight or is it curving?

Straight or curving?

Can you remember which things move **straight** and which things **curve**?

Index

Notes for adults

The *How Do Things Move?* series provides young children with a first opportunity to learn about motion. Each book encourages children to notice and ask questions about the types of movement they see around them. The following Early Learning Goals are relevant to the series:

Knowledge and understanding of the world
• Find out about and identify some features of living things and objects
• Ask questions about why things happen and how things work
• Show an interest in the world in which they live
• Encourage use of evaluative and comparative language

These books will also help children extend their vocabulary, as they will hear some new words. Since words are used in context in the book this should enable young children to gradually incorporate them into their own vocabulary.

Follow-up activities
• Reinforce the concepts of straight and curved by asking your child to identify three objects in the room with curves, and three objects with straight lines.
• Encourage your child to think further about moving in a straight or curved line by asking them to decide which would be quicker to get from A to B. Then get them to test their theory by running across the room.